SAARLAND

Text by
Wilfried Burr

Photos by
Roland Schiffler

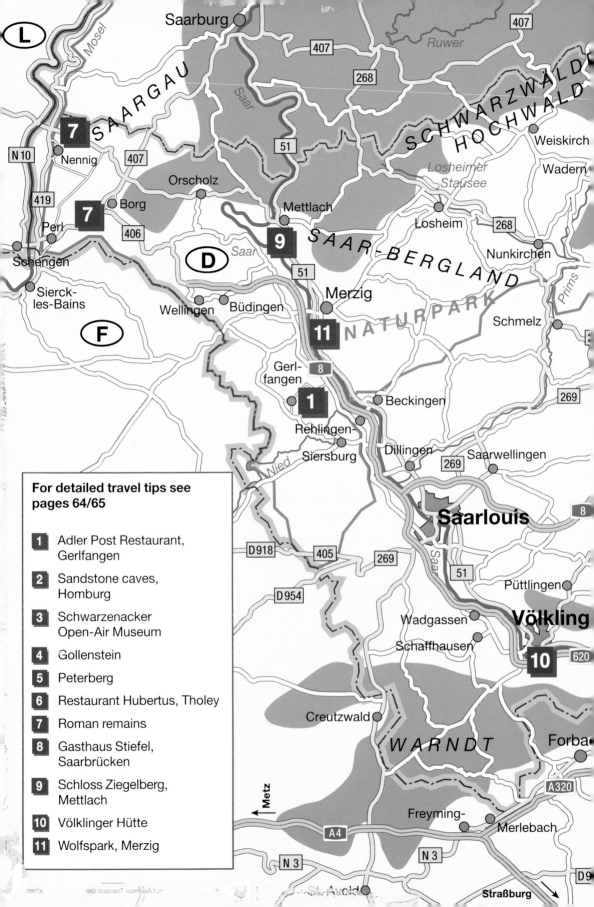

Saarburg

Mosel

L

SAARGAU

N 10

7

Nennig

407

Orscholz

Borg

7

406

Perl

419

Schengen

Sierck-les-Bains

D

Saar

Wellingen

Büdingen

F

Ruwer

407

407

268

51

SCHWARZWÄLD
HOCHWALD

Weiskirch

Wadern

Losheimer
Stausee

Mettlach

9

Losheim

268

Nunkirchen

SAAR-BERGLAND

Merzig

11

NATURPARK

Prims

Schmelz

269

Gerl-fangen

8

1

Rehlingen-
Siersburg

Nied

Beckingen

Dillingen

Saarwellingen

269

Schmelz

8

**For detailed travel tips see
pages 64/65**

1 Adler Post Restaurant,
Gerlfangen

2 Sandstone caves,
Homburg

3 Schwarzenacker
Open-Air Museum

4 Gollenstein

5 Peterberg

6 Restaurant Hubertus, Tholey

7 Roman remains

8 Gasthaus Stiefel,
Saarbrücken

9 Schloss Ziegelberg,
Mettlach

10 Völklinger Hütte

11 Wolfspark, Merzig

D918

405

269

Saarlouis

Saar

51

Püttlingen

Völkling

D954

Wadgassen

Schaffhausen

10

620

Metz

Creutzwald

WARNDT

Forba

A320

Freyming-

Merlebach

A4

N 3

N 3

St-Avold

Straßburg

D9

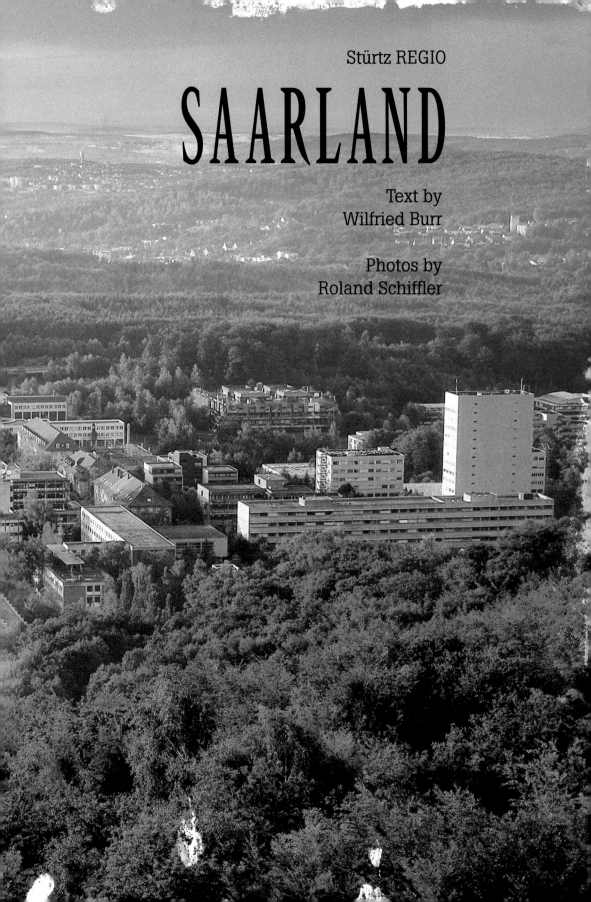

Stürtz REGIO

SAARLAND

Text by
Wilfried Burr

Photos by
Roland Schiffler

Top front cover:
bend in the River
Saar at Orscholz.
Bottom front cover
(from left to right):
Saarland miner in
traditional costume,
the Ludwigskirche
in Saarbrücken
and the interior of
St. Wendalinus
Basilica.

Page 4/5:
the University of
the Saarland
in Saarbrücken's
city forest.
Page 8/9:
Saarbrücken's palace
in all its night-time
splendour.
The modern centre
section designed
by Gottfried Böhm
stands in vivid
contrast to the
Baroque wings of
the building.

Back cover:
the Völklinger Hütte
with the town hall
and power station.

The Authors:

Wilfried Burr, born in Wadern in 1937, lives in Nonnweiler and is a long-standing editor for the *Saarbrücker Zeitung*. Since 1994 he heads the travel and local history departments.

Roland Schiffler, born in Saarbrücken in 1963, studied geography in Saarbrücken and Berlin. He has been working as a photographer since 1995 and as a photographic designer since 1997.

Credits

Photos:
Archiv für Kunst und Geschichte, Berlin:
p. 38, p. 39, p. 60 bottom.
Wolfgang Klauke, Saarbrücken: p. 22 centre.
Filmfestival Max Ophüls Preis: P. 22 bottom.

© 2004 Verlagshaus Würzburg GmbH & Co.KG, Würzburg

Editing: Carina Orf, Mainbernheim
Design: Förster Illustration & Grafik, Rimpar
Cartography: Kartendienst Andreas Toscano
del Banner, München
Repro: Universitätsdruckerei H. Stürtz AG,
Würzburg
Translation: Ruth Chitty, Schweppenhausen
Printed and edited by the
Offizin Andersen Nexö, Leipzig

ISBN 3-8003-1112-7

CONTENTS

Living on the 10
Border to France
Portrait of a
Landscape

Vicus, Villa et 30
Taberna
Archaeological Finds
in the Saarland

"Haubdsach', ... 44
gudd gess..."
Culinary
Saar Specialities

Good Luck! 60
Mining
in the Saarland

Chronological Table 66
Saarland
History
in a Nutshell

22 ...Avant-Garde to the Fore
The Max Ophüls Festival
and Perspectives du
théâtre français

38 ....A Political Bone
of Contention
The Struggle for Power
over the Saarland

52 ....Made in the Saarland
Ceramics Manufacturers
Villeroy & Boch

64 ....At a Glance
Tips for Trips
in the Saarland

69 ....Index
The Saarland
from A – Z

LIVING ON THE BORDER TO FRANCE

Geographically squeezed into a corner between France and Germany, pushed politically back and forth time and again, the Saarland knows how to stand up for itself. More than once the people of this region have been considered the bone of contention, worried by two neighbouring powers. Constantly being forced to assert themselves has made fighters of the Saarländer.

Saarland idyll on the other side of the border. The River Blies flows into the Saar at the little town of Sarreguemines (Saargemünd) in Lorraine. In the background: an old earthenware factory.

Fight yet enjoy life – this combination is the credo the Saarländer have thought up for themselves, a variation on the French *savoir-vivr*e.

"Saarvoir-vivre" is neither French nor 100 % German,

but somewhere between the two. Writer Ludwig Harig, a Saarländer through and through, expounds: "Living and being capable of living, live and let live; that's life the Saarland way."

Roughly translated, one rather flogged local phrase claims that with a good meal inside you things will run more smoothly ("Haubdsach' gudd gess! Geschafft han mir dann schnell!"). Non-locals could interpret this as a sign of an exaggeratedly happy-go-lucky attitude towards things. It isn't – it's a serious battle cry aimed at combating melancholy tendencies. Eat well and the burden of day-to-day life is easier to bear. The Saarland burden is a heavy one. Mining and the iron and steel industry, the economic cornerstones of bygone decades and centuries, have been forced into the defensive. They have radically dwindled in importance; redundancies and unemployment are dull reality for many of the province's inhabitants. These depressing truths bring out the Saarland fighting spirit, call for defiant revolt against resignation and worry. Defiance is the key word – the Saarland vernacular even has its own expression for it: "Grad seläds".

Despite all the economic traumas, native Saarländer not only want their small Bundesland to remain habitable; they want it to become even more attractive. The same goes for part-time Saarländer, for

those who spend a few days or even weeks in what's known as the Saar-Lor-Lux (Saarland- Lorraine- Luxembourg) area. Most of them leave for home with a positive impression in their minds, the image of the "Saarland smoke hole", possibly in their luggage when they arrived,

dumped on the slag heap of errors. That doesn't mean that the Saarland is devoid of sad images; there are plenty of moribund collieries, rusty blast furnaces and sooty chimneys. But the Saarland is also one of Germany's greenest states, with one of the largest areas of forest.

The Saarland is a land of contrast.

The scenic make-up of the roughly 1,000 square miles of Saarland is extremely diverse. Three very different types of landscape shape the region: the Hunsrück with the Schwarzwälder Hochwald, the Lorraine Palatinate stratum with its fertile *Gau* lands along the Saar, Moselle and Blies rivers, and the Saar-Nahe mountains. The north is characterised by large expanses of forest and rolling hills which border on the Southern Hunsrück. The Saar Valley is flanked by the Saargau and the Bliesgau, the Warndt and Kirkel Forest.

Tradition and modernity in neighbourly harmony: in the mining village of Göttelborn mining past meets mining present. Old pit houses next to a contemporary winding tower.

The Saarland's "sovereign territory" includes part of the Upper Moselle where wine has been cultivated since Roman times. The scenic high point of the Saarland is without doubt the famous, photogenic bow in the river between the spa town of Orscholz and ceramics centre Mettlach. Over millions of years the waters of the Saar have eroded the rock, layer by layer, forcing the river's course and producing the Saarland's showpiece. This fantastic natural phenomenon can be viewed in all its splendour from Cloef viewpoint near Orscholz. Below, pleasure boats chug back and forth along the river from Merzig to Saarburg in Rhineland-Palatinate via Mettlach.

History in the Saarland goes back a long way.

The Gollenstein obelisk near the Baroque town of Blieskastel, where Kneipp administered his famous cures, is from the Neolithic period and around 4,000 years old. At the beginning of the Second World War the stone was pulled down by the German Wehrmacht "to prevent it from becoming an enemy target", whereupon it split into four pieces. The Gollenstein wasn't re-erected in its original form until 1951. Visitors can go right up to

the 22-foot menhir, the largest in Central Europe,

and explore it first-hand, as they can with the stone's smaller counterparts, the 16-foot Spellenstein in Rentrisch and 6,000-year-old "Obelix" in Walhausen.

The Celtic fortifications on Dollberg Hill near Otzenhausen are much younger. The enormous hillside settlement has been well preserved and is thought to have been built in the first century B.C. The earthworks are one-and-a-half miles long and made of over eight million cubic feet of stone. The Treverian count who sought refuge from the Romans here with his followers was probably Caesar's bitter opponent Indutiomarus. Historians are still arguing about who was the first king of this Celtic castle. One thing they agree on, however, is whom the steps giving access to the north wall were built for: in 1836 Frederick William III, King of Prussia,

Romans and Celts were not the only civilisations to leave their mark on the Saarland.

Their successors have also bequeathed many an heirloom, in the form of castles and palaces, Gothic and Baroque residences, churches and chapels, old farmhouses and French fortresses. The Thirty Years' War carved a bloody scar across the land, like the other Franco-German conflicts after it, not to mention two world wars. In the last 200 years the region has changed hands eight times.

There are two commodities, however, which managed to retain some

Heathen mysteries: Mithraism also found a home in the Saarland, as this temple on Halberghang in Saarbrücken proves.

The Romans were also active here before the Christianisation of the area, as shown by the wallpaper in the Roman villa at Nennig (right).

had his "humble servants" fashion them for his visit.

form of constancy throughout the identity crisis of Saarland history: trade and industry. Arts and crafts, agriculture and viniculture, iron mining and processing were initiated here by the Romans. In the middle of the last century mining and the steel and glass industries (in St. Ingbert and Fenne), which had enjoyed only rather modest beginnings, caused a tremendous flourish in local activity.

In a short space of time a multitude of towns and villages sprang up,

greatly changing the face of the surrounding countryside. Coal mines and steel works have determined

fred Henrich smugly claimed that "today the Sun King's nephew reigns here". In the same breath he proclaimed his district town the "secret capital" of the province. Locals allege Henrich made good his claim; the many friendly pubs and good restaurants in the picturesque old part of town are not only a positive urban contribution but also draw inhabitants from the "real" state capital, Saarbrücken.

Pictorial documentation of life in the Saarland (from left to right): the old blast furnace in Neunkirchen, a wire pull at the Saarstahl steel works in Burbach and the gloved hands of a qualified miner holding a miniature pick at a miners' festival at the Maybach pit.

the world of work in the Saarland over many centuries – until very recently. The steel industry, for example, was given an early boost in 1685, when Sun King Louis XIV, who also initiated the building of the fortress in Saarlouis, gave steel works expert Marquis de Lénoncourt permission "to erect iron, steel and smelting works on [the king's] estate in Dillingen".

Saarlouis is often called the "secret capital" of the Saarland. The town, whose French flair is more pronounced than Saarbrücken's, was constructed as a riverside fortification by Louis XIV in 1685. Three centuries later town mayor Dr. Man-

Many of the towns in the Saarland are bursting with contrast. Saarbrücken, for example, is a lively confluence of the Baroque past and the pulsating present. Someone much taken by Saarbrücken as long ago as 1770 was Johann Wolfgang von Goethe. "We reached Saarbrück via Saargemünd, and the small royal capital was a shimmer of light in this rocky, wooded country. The town, small and hilly, yet elegantly embellished by the last count, immediately makes a pleasant impression, as the houses are all painted greyish white, their varying heights a multifarious sight", wrote the prince among poets.

The heart of Saarbrücken is the St. Johanner Markt.

The pedestrian zone is a hive of colourful activity, especially on market days. From spring to autumn the cheery hustle and bustle inside and outside the smart watering holes goes on until well into the night. You shouldn't just visit the St. Johanner Markt for a gossip and a pint, however – there's also plenty for the eye to behold. The oldest houses on

branch of the Bruch brewery. Museum relics from its beer-brewing past are on display. There is, of course, more on offer at the Stiefel brewery than just a few museum pieces; they still brew their own beer according to the traditional recipe and will happily serve you a freshly pulled pint of it!

For those who are less drawn by the cities and their cultural heritage, perhaps the surrounding country-

Enjoying a warm summer evening on St. Johanner Markt in Saarbrücken (left).

the square, with their Late Gothic and Renaissance windows, are from the 16th century.

The square's distinguishing feature is its Baroque fountain from 1760, designed by Friedrich Joachim Stengel. The obelisk is crowned by the rose of St. Johann positioned above a vase, once an independent village which together with Alt-Saarbrücken and Burbach-Malstatt was affiliated to the city of Saarbrücken in 1909.

A jewel among the taverns on the Markt is the Stiefel Bräu. Probably Saarbrücken's oldest pub, it was built in 1718 and was the parent

side is a better place to unwind. Bostal Lake in the St. Wendeler Land is a major attraction from spring to autumn.

The Saarland's largest inland water accommodates keen sailors,

surfers and beach-volleyball players. In the heat of summer bathers join the merry throng. Losheim's lake lies in beautiful surroundings and also permits various kinds of water sports, but fjord-like Primstal Lake near Nonnweiler health resort is a no-go area for aqueous activities. "Peaceful, eco-friendly relaxation"

Bostal Lake in the St. Wendeler Land is territorial water for sailors and surfers. In the water-sports season hobby seamen and professional captains have priority (right).

is the maxim issued by the municipality of Nonnweiler which forbids any kind of water sport on its 247 acres of reservoir. Cyclists and hikers, however, are welcome and can peddle or meander along the grand lakeside tracks to their heart's content.

The neighbouring district is also well suited to those seeking peace and quiet.

The district town of St. Wendel is encircled by beautiful hills and forest.

The town's centrepiece is the monumental St. Wendalinus Basilica. It gets its name from the son of an Irish or Scottish king who relinquished the comforts of his royal existence to become a simple shepherd near Tholey. There are many legends surrounding the work and wonders of St. Wendalinus (554 – 617); his grave is the target of numerous pilgrimages. In Southern Germany Wendalinus is the patron saint of farmers, cattle breeders and their animals.

Art forges a link between the districts of St. Wendel and Merzig-Wadern, between culture and nature. St. Wendeler Land's Sculpture Trail (Skulpturenstraße), erected amidst fields and meadows in 1971, is mirrored by its neighbour's Stones along the Border Project (Steine an der Grenze). The latter, which sparked off a sculpture symposium near Merzig in 1986, aims to "bear witness to the art of our day and age and to the understanding which transcends national boundaries". The result is an impressive collation of plastic art dotted along the border between Büdingen and

Serene waters: Primstal Lake near Nonnweiler in the north of the Saarland is a place for calm reflection, for water sports are not permitted on the 247 acres of reservoir. Hikers and cyclists appreciate the peace and quiet.

Wellingen in the Saarland and Ritzing and Launstroff in Lorraine.

As you can see, the spectrum of activities for those travelling to the

selves, stationed in the very heart of Europe. Former German president Richard von Weizsäcker offered succinct words on the subject: "People here are

good Saarländer, good Europeans and good neighbours."

A miner at his window in the mining town of Maybach after a hard day's work (right).

Contrasts: the sculpture in front of the Moderne Galerie in Saarbrücken (top left), footballing youngsters at their one-two premiere and traditional costume in Losheim (centre).

Saarland is broad. From the bustling towns of Saarbrücken and Saarlouis to the traces left behind by Celts and Romans and back to the many sports activities offered by lakes, forests and hills, there is something for everyone in the Saarland. You can even sail by pleasure boat from Saarbrücken to Saargemünd (Sarreguemines) in Lorraine, for example, or try your luck on the horses. The race course at Güdingen's Saarwiesen, which pulls huge crowds of keen French and German betters up to half a dozen times a year, encroaches on French territory. It traverses the borders like the Saarländer themselves.

One thing Herr von Weizsäcker forgot to mention in his Saarland laudation is that Saarländer are also sociable souls. Festivals are celebrated all year round in the merry old land of Saar. For a real taste of Saarvoir-vivre, try Emmes (the gourmet festival in Saarlouis), the Moselle wine festival in Perl–Nennig, the Wendalinus Festwoche in St. Wendel and the huge Viezfest in Merzig. Rendezvous with the Saarland and enjoy. *Prost* – and *guten Appetit!* ■

The Staatstheater: Saarbrücken's temple of the muses on the banks of the Saar (top). The state chancellery: these buildings are part of the ensemble of government buildings on Ludwigsplatz fashioned by architect Stengel.

The chic of youth: smart hats (top) and sociable moments out in the sun at the St. Johanner Fountain (centre) and in front of Saarbrücken's mining offices (bottom).

Treasured relics of old Saarbrücken: St. Arnual's Collegiate Church (top left), whose more important artefacts include the memorial slabs dedicated to John III and his wives (bottom left) and the tomb of the Prince of Nassau-Saarbrücken (top centre).

Old Saarbrücken's landmark is the monumental Ludwigskirche on the square of the same name (main photo). The interior of the Baroque church has excellent acoustics for the organ (top).

AVANT-GARDE TO THE FORE

The Saarland has an exciting arts scene, offering a world of sophisticated entertainment and inspiring creativity.

The state province offers a very high standard of theatre

and draws the culture-loving crowds with its broad spectrum of top-class events. Examples are the Max Ophüls Festival and the Perspectives du théâtre français Festival, whose performers confirm that the arts in Saarbrücken have a strong leaning towards the European and the avant-garde.

The namesake of the Ophüls Festival, film director Max Ophüls, whose home town was Saarbrücken.

Max Ophüls, from whom the yearly film festival gets its appellation, was born in Saarbrücken on May 6, 1902. He enjoyed little success as an actor. His rise to fame came as a director of films such as *Der Reigen* (The Roundelay, 1950) and *Lola Montez* (1955). He filmed in Germany, Austria, Switzerland and England and in 1933 left Germany to work in Paris, Rome and Hollywood. He died of a heart condition in Hamburg in 1957.

Saarbrücken has brought back its lost son in name at least; in January 1997 the Max Ophüls Prize for the best German-speaking director from Germany, Switzerland, Austria or Luxembourg was awarded for the 18th time. The film competition has established itself as

a platform for young film-makers and also young actors.

In 1997 the jury had to pick the winner destined to receive the award worth DM 60,000 (ca. £20,000) from 18 films. That must have been quite a challenging task, for the Max Ophüls Festival has since its birth been considered the meeting place of the German avant-garde. Here, eccentricity is the order of the day.

Unconventionality also comes up trumps at Saarbrücken's French theatre festival (Perspectives for short). In 1997 the event had a round birthday; it turned 20. When Jochen Zoerner-Erb, dramaturge at the Staatstheater, publicly announced his idea for a festival of French theatre in Saarbrücken in 1978, he found a willing patron and keen supporter in young mayor Oskar Lafontaine.

In disused factories or at open-air events on the St. Johanner Markt spectators sit glued to a rather different kind of theatre:

experimental and spontaneous, it's a far cry from the often static forms of classical theatre

most of us are familiar with. It's avant-garde to the fore at the Max Ophüls Festival and at Perspectives, lavishly splashing Saarbrücken's cultural calendar with an entire palette of bizarre colour. ■

Young artists stage performances of modern and contemporary open-air theatre at the Perspectives (top two pictures).

The yearly festival has long enjoyed a good reputation and is well received by Saarbrücken audiences (bottom).

The Saar is truly European and without frontiers. In French Sarreguemines the beautiful river glides under the Allies' Bridge (main photo) and past the gateway to the old earthenware factory (bottom right). In Germany's Saarbrücken it flows under the Alte Brücke, with the state parliament in the background (top left), and past the reconstruction of a historic crane (top right).

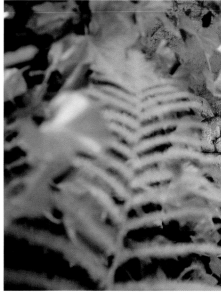

Life is great when the sun's shining (here in Blies-kastel, top left). The Schlangen-brunnen with its snakes on Alter Markt was erected in honour of Napoleon in 1804. A pilgrimage chapel dedicated to the Holy Cross stands in the Capuchin monastery park (top centre).

Prehistoric stones rise up tall and powerful in the landscape. The 22-foot Gollenstein near Blieskastel (top right) is the largest menhir in Central Europe and, like the Stiefel ("boot") near Rentrisch (main photo), is a popular destination with hikers.

St. Steven's in Blieskastel-Böckweiler is 1,000 years old (top centre).

Gustavsburg Castle near Homburg, built in 1721 and now a museum (main photo), and the round Annahof Restaurant in the village of Niederwürzbach (top left) are of a considerably younger vintage.

The burial chapel in Bischmisheim (above) shows the wonderful architectural hand of Karl Friedrich Schinkel. The master of the Prussian style has left several traces of his creativity in Saarbrücken.

VICUS, VILLA ET TABERNA

The Roman Festival in Schwarzenacker (top left) transports its onlookers and participants back to the past to which these amphorae bear witness (right).

One summer's day in 1991 a farmer ploughing his high-lying field near Oberlöstern in the Northern Saarland hit upon a historical hindrance. Celtic? Roman? Or both? The archaeological verdict: two Roman graves with Celtic markings from the 2nd century A.D.

This is just one of many examples. Under Saarland soil slumber the remnants of early history;

the probability of unearthing subterranean riches here is extremely high.

In past decades numerous remains, some of them up to two thousand years old, have been excavated from the sites of archaic settlements in Germany's most southwesterly state. Is the Saarland a Gallo-Roman treasure-trove?

Many archaeological finds point towards a Gallo-Roman past for the Saarland. In the 1st century B.C. Gaius Julius Caesar, the great statesman and famous Roman general, managed to conquer Gaul – which included what is now the Saarland – for Rome. The main route between the two Roman metropolises of Trier and Metz ran right through the Saargau.

One of the Roman centres of trade and transportation is thought to have been the *vicus* at Bliesbruck

The past reconstructed: houses and pillars at Schwarzenacker Open-Air Museum remind us of the region's Roman inhabitants.

(now the European Archaeological Park of Bliesbruck-Reinheim) which sprawls unhindered across the French-German border in both directions. Here archaeologists have discovered a Gallo-Roman city, with impressive baths and a trades and crafts quarter on French terrain and a Roman villa, farm and Celtic princesses' grave on the German side.

Roman mosaic floor this side of the Alps. Approximately three million pieces of stone have been arranged in a rectangle ca. 32 feet by 49 feet depicting hunting scenes and fighting gladiators.

The Roman villa in the forest near Borg demonstrates just how comfortable Roman baths were. The reconstructed villa features

a bathing area over 4,300 square feet in size with warm, cold and tepid baths.

After their relaxing spell in the water the Romans probably sat down to a glass of wine in the adjoining *taberna*. This has been

You can marvel at an ancient heating system, a hypocaust, at Reinheim-

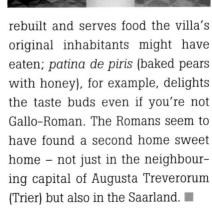

If we cross the Saar and head northwest to the Moselle Valley we will find more evidence of Roman culture. Roman "Saarländer" chose the German slopes of the Moselle to plant their vines; finds prove they were the first wine-growers in the area around Schloss Berg. Not far from the castle is Nennig, whose claim to fame is its reconstructed Roman villa with the biggest, best-preserved

rebuilt and serves food the villa's original inhabitants might have eaten; *patina de piris* (baked pears with honey), for example, delights the taste buds even if you're not Gallo-Roman. The Romans seem to have found a second home sweet home – not just in the neighbouring capital of Augusta Treverorum (Trier) but also in the Saarland. ∎

Bliesbruck Archaeological Park (top left). The Roman villa in Borg (left) with its cold bath (centre) and the mosaic floor in Nennig (right) show us just how comfortable life was for the area's early inhabitants.

The blast furnace and old water tower in Neunkirchen are the only remnants of a thriving mining community.

Neunkirchen's industrial mementos: this statue of an iron founder has come to symbolise the town. The former water tower is now a cinema proffering on-screen excitement on a daily basis (bottom).

The only value this gear shaft still has, set against the backdrop of Neunkirchen, is as a museum piece. It adorns the historic mining path which runs by the town on the River Blies.

The Lady Altar in Gothic St. Wendalinus Basilica (top) is a peaceful place of prayer for the church's pilgrims. Despite the stylistic discrepancies in the choir and nave the interior of the hall church with its net vault presents a uniform ensemble.

St. Wendalinus's stone sarcophagus is decorated with artistic figures and stands in the basilica dedicated to him. Numerous legends are attached to St. Wendalinus. In Southern Germany he is the patron saint of farmers and their animals.

The basilica dominates St. Wendel. Markets are often held on the church square surrounding the mighty edifice which attracts numerous pilgrims each year from all over Southern Germany. On warm summer days the town's restaurateurs set up chairs and tables around the church for visitors eager to taste the local cuisine.

Architectural gems and the charm of the countryside (from top left to right): the historic market place in Ottweiler, the Johann Adams Mühle farm museum in Theley and Schaumberg Hill near Tholey.

Wide, open, windy countryside: view from Schaumberg, the Saarland's local mountain, of Theley and the Hochwald Forest (main photo). Bostal Lake offers watery idyll, here with its pedal boats moored up for the evening. By day the lake is alive with the shouts and splashes of bathers and those taking time out. The wooded shores are ideal terrain for long walks.

A POLITICAL BONE OF CONTENTION

Because of its geographical position, squashed in between France and Germany, and its wealth of coal, the Saarland has been something of a political shunting yard several times during its history. More than once the people of the Saar have fallen under the jurisdiction of the French government, only finally becoming part of Germany in the second half of the 20th century.

Die Saar, la Sarre – sometimes German, sometimes French, these are the names of a river caught up in a long-standing political battle.

The Saarland found itself in the midst of a national tug of war after the two world wars, for example.

The Treaty of Versailles in 1920 handed over the Saar mines to France,

Saar plebiscite in 1935. Those too ill or handicapped to make it to the polling station alone were carried to their vote.

placed French neighbours in leading positions and put the administration of the Saar Territory under the trust of the League of Nations for 15 years. Only after this period expired were the inhabitants allowed to choose which country they wanted to belong to by way of a plebiscite.

As might be expected, relations between the ruling French powers and the oppressed Saarländer were not always peaceful. Patriotism and the rebellious spirit were strong, with nationalistic slogans, such as "Heim ins Reich", and the secret *Deutsch ist die Saar* anthem being spouted at every opportunity. The flames of emotion burned brighter from 1930 onwards. A good 90 % of the valid voting slips filled in at the plebiscite on January 13, 1935, chose to return to the fatherland. At the time, National Socialist voters were still in the minority, something

they compensated for by playing their propaganda machine loud and long. On March 1, 1935, the League of Nations surrendered the Saar Territory to the German Reich. The same afternoon, Adolf Hitler took to the political stage in Saarbrücken,

and his followers hoped that the Saar statute would be accepted, which caused many violent disturbances in the months preceding the vote. On October 23, 1955,

the Saarländer again trotted along to the polling stations;

accompanied by a huge parade of members and sympathisers of the Nazi Party.

Ten years later, after Germany's defeat in the Second World War, America and then France again took control of the Saar. Its status was not that of a territory occupied by France; it remained politically "autonomous" but was under French control on account of its customs and currency union with the Grande Nation.

The Saar sent its own team to the Olympic Games in Helsinki

and in 1954 actually played against the German football team in the qualifying rounds for the World Cup, the scores being 0 : 3 and 1 : 3. In the same year, France and Germany signed an agreement which would give the Saar "European statute under the Western European Union", to be decided by plebiscite. Saarland prime minister Johannes Hoffmann

67.7% threw out the proposed statute. The Saarland was politically and economically (re)united with Germany; in 1959 the borders between Germany and the Saar were dismantled. Since then there hasn't been a political bone of contention in sight. The Saarland illustrates that European co-operation works better here than in any other state in Germany. ∎

The Saar returns "home" to Germany once again. Federal Minister of Germany Heinrich von Brentano (centre) and France's foreign secretary Christian Pineau (right) sign the Saar contracts on October 27, 1956, in Luxembourg.

Impressions from the north of the Saarland (from top left to right): you can slip and slide to your heart's content on south-west Germany's longest summer toboggan run (almost 3,000 feet long) on Peterberg. This old farmhouse with its halcyon garden in Weiskirchen seems to stem from the days of yore. Schloss Dagstuhl near Wadern (main photo) was built around 1750. Paintings by Countess Octavie de Lasalle von Louisenthal still adorn the palace chapel.

Previous double spread: hang-glider on Peterberg near Braunshausen.

"HAUBDSACH', GUDD GESS..."

Hoorische are a typical Saarland speciality.

Looking at all the centuries of co-operation and conflict between France and Germany, it's hardly surprising that neighbouring France's *haute cuisine* has greatly influenced

the contents of Saarland pots and pans.

France has always been and still is omnipresent – on both sides of the "great" divide.

Thus gourmets on holiday in the Saarland can but need not necessarily cross the almost invisible border to find a *carte du jour* offering the classics of French cooking.

Lots of Saarländer are fans of French food, yet the majority loves solid home cooking, preferring to

whet their appetite with their top local dishes. These are dominated by a single tuber: the potato. Whether as *Hoorische, Gefillde* or *Dibbelabbes*, no self-respecting Saarland menu would be without it.

Hoorische are potato dumplings with a rather hairy appearance.

(otherwise known in Germany as *Klöße*). "Through cooking the fibres of the grated raw potato stick out slightly, like a crew cut", is how one local cookbook writer describes them. *Hoorische*, also known in some regions as *Buwespatze*, are excellent accompaniments to various roasts. But they also taste good eaten with a cream and bacon sauce and salad or with sauerkraut. *Gefillde* are also potato dumplings, but these are filled with mince and have a spicy flavour. The third variation, *Dibbelabbes*, is a huge potato fritter and also a hot favourite with the local inhabitants.

When speaking of regional dishes in the Saarland, there's one which absolutely must be included: *Lyoner*, the local version of pork sausage. Saarländer are very creative with

It's also common knowledge that Saarland father Oskar Lafontaine is a man who likes good food, and through this

a change is slowly being brought about in Saarland cuisine

in favour of "creative, tasty Saarland cooking", to quote Koop. If political discussions in Bonn aren't as successful as Lafontaine and his colleagues. would like, they can always go down to the kitchen to Heinz-Peter Koop and in unison chant the Saarland credo: "Haubdsach', gudd gess..." ■

it; from kebabs to goulash there are countless variations and permutations which even connoisseurs find hard to resist.

Saarland's top chef, Heinz-Peter Koop, has the following to say about *Lyoner*:

"Lyoner still tastes good, but the proverbial Saarland Lyoner mentality is slowly abating."

The trend is gradually moving away from heavy, substantial food to lighter, more digestible meals based on traditional recipes. For it's a known fact that heavy meals make you sluggish and lethargic, qualities the Saarland faction Heinz-Peter Koop cooks for at the Bonn government definitely doesn't need.

With its various districts, Perl on the Upper Moselle is the only area where wine is cultivated in the Saarland. Schloss Saarfels is also included in this vinicultural region (right).

Alcoholic grape juice can be savoured at Weinstube Hauck in Saarbrücken (top left). The Merzig region's liquid speciality is cider or "apple wine", with cider queens being chosen and crowned at regular intervals (bottom left).

45

*The Hochwald
Forest area
around Wadern
is ideal territory
for riders.*

*In hibernation:
Löstertal between
Wadern and
Nonnweiler is not
only attractive
in the clutches of
winter (left).*

*Following double
spread: the jewel
of the Saarland is
the spectacular
bow in the Saar,
best seen from
Cloef viewpoint
near Orscholz.*

Full sail ahead! Between spring and autumn Losheim's lake is an El Dorado for water-sports fans and bathers (main photo). Hikers prefer the rural environs of Waldhölzbach (top

The old Benedictine monastery at Mettlach (main photo) sprawls majestic on the banks of the River Saar. It is now the headquarters of ceramics manufacturers Villeroy & Boch. Homo Ceramicus (bottom right) has his place in the abbey park. Mettlach's landmark is the Alter Turm (below). Other historic highlights in the surrounding area include Schloss Berg near Nennig (top left) and Burg Montclair, shrouded in legend (top right).

MADE IN THE SAARLAND

Top left: the Boch and Gallo coat of arms. Right: bust of Eugen von Boch.

It came to light off the coast of Newfoundland. In the wreck of the *Titanic*, which sank in 1912, divers exploring the watery remains of the luxury liner found tiles made in Mettlach in the Saarland. The swimming pool, bathrooms and kitchen had been decorated with products by ceramics manufacturer Villeroy & Boch. The porcelain giant claims it's possible that the tableware and ceramic sanitary facilities may also have come from their factory.

In 1998 Villeroy & Boch will be 250.

Their professional liaison with the *Titanic* is just one of many chapters in the company's history books. Other auspicious events include their mosaic floor for Cologne Cathedral in 1894 and extensive tiling, still in an excellent state of preservation, installed at the Bolshoy Theatre in Moscow in 1904. Around the turn of the century the Russians came up with a new generic term for stoneware tiles, "Mettlachkije Plitki" – recognition for V&B dating back to the time of the tsars.

Villeroy & Boch's path to world success spans two-and-a-half centuries. Potteries had long provided the Saarland with an economic backcloth – finds from the Roman period prove this – and it was a pottery which marked Villeroy & Boch's modest beginnings. In 1748 François Boch owned a pottery in the village of Audun-le-Tiche in Lorraine. Almost a century later Boch merged with fellow manufacturer Villeroy, their bond being strengthened by marriage between the two families a few years later. The centre of their activities, unofficially termed the "ceramics capital", was Mettlach on the Lower Saar.

Unique: the last copper engraver working in industry at V & B.

The traditional company has its headquarters in an old Benedictine monastery, but production is not limited to this prestigious location. The world concern now has over 20 sites in Germany, France, Luxembourg, Italy, Holland, Austria, Hungary and Rumania. Their range of products includes tableware, wall and floor tiles, sanitary installations

ceramics were and are now produced and used in an informative and entertaining way.

The true treasures of the ceramic world

are not in the monastery but at the Schloss Ziegelberg Museum. Stoneware and porcelain from two cen-

V & B's "white rose" design is diligently painted by hand (top left). V & B's best pieces of porcelain are on display in the Keravision (top right).

and bathroom furnishings. In 1990 the family business became a listed company.

Creativity is today considered one of V & B's strongest points.

Examples of past ingenuity are on display at the Mettlach monastery. The Chapter House has a special electronics set-up (called the Keravision) which shows the visitor how

turies can be marvelled at in the splendid rooms of the *Gründerzeit* villa where Adolf von Boch used to reside. The permanent collection comprises no less than 9,000 precious pieces, and there are also changing exhibitions featuring ceramic masterpieces by modern artists. The exhibits don't, however, include items rescued from the bowels of the *Titanic*... ∎

Ceramic products leaving the glazing kiln (bottom left). The company headquarters boast wall mosaics depicting scenes of Hamburg (bottom centre) and – in true Saarland fashion – a miner (bottom right).

The towers and steeples of St. Peter's rise up majestically above the roofs of Merzig (top left). Überherrn's local landmark is Teufelsburg Castle (centre left). Niedaltdorf has some fascinating dripstone caves (bottom left).

The Stones along the Border Project in the Saargau near Merzig is a collection of artistic sculptures (top right and main photo) dotted about the countryside. Its counterpart in the St. Wendeler Land is the Sculpture Trail.

Saarlouis, the "secret capital" of the Saarland. The Ludwigskirche acts as an intermediary between ancient and modern architecture (main photo). French field marshal Michel Ney (top left) is an important figure for the town; he even has a restaurant named after him (top right).

Centre right: a sculpture in contemporary guise; plane trees cast their shade on the former parade ground (bottom right).

Following double spread: the Völklinger Hütte, a UNESCO World Heritage Site, with the town hall tower and power station.

GOOD LUCK!

Mining on the Saar: the coal cutter at the Göttelborn mine (top left) is still in operation.

In the 19th century being a miner-farmer was a common form of occupation above and below ground along the Saar.

Coal and steel have provided generations of Saarländer with their main source of income.

Weiher Power Station (top right) near Göttelborn and Quierschied is to stay open. The future for the mining community, however, remains bleak.

A living hard-earned; the underground working day at the end of the 19th century was 12 hours long, extremely laborious and paid only around DM 3 – DM 3.50 (just over £ 1.00). This, together with the meagre harvest the miner-farmer

selves also look back to a long tradition; archaeological finds show that settlers long before the Romans extracted iron here.

Out of the many collieries in the Saarland, only a few are still in operation. Unemployment figures are on the increase.

One of the pits still open is Göttelborn;

Soot and smog. The (translated) title of this wood engraving from 1867 is "From the Saarland Coal Basin: View of Neunkirchen".

managed to yield from his crops, had to feed a family of four to ten. In 1927 two thirds of those in employment in the Saarland worked in the mining and iron and steel industries like their fathers and grandfathers before them. The industries them-

coal is still mined here, albeit in humble quantities, and the mining tradition still maintained. But not for much longer. From the turn of the millennium on the coalfield's "black gold" will have to remain in its subterranean dungeon; at the end of 1999 Göttelborn is to close the pit. It's no longer profitable to keep it running. With its closure more jobs and another segment of Saarland tradition disappear. What will happen to the colliery – another museum, perhaps? Like many other Saarland mines? Like the Saarland Mining Museum (Bergbaumuseum) at Bexbach with its mining shafts and tunnels, the historic pits at Frankenholz, Nordfeld and St. Ingbert and the visitors' mine at Düppenweiler?

All that's left for them to do is to document the working lives of the pitmen – in museum form.

Like mining, the steel industry, once a thriving branch of the economy, has also fallen prey to recession. The old Völklinger Hütte, for example, was closed in 1986, but has had a positive rebirth.

It was made a UNESCO World Heritage Site

in 1994 because of the perfection and unique quality of the complex. The iron and steel works with its blast furnace, coking plant, glass

blower unit and machinery from 1900 – 1913 has been refurbished to accommodate tourist day-trippers and the entertainments industry. The mighty industrial cathedral on the banks of the Saar, heavily crudded with rust, is a monument to a branch of industry which has almost completely disappeared, at the same time providing a venue for arts events. Cultural virtue is made of industrial necessity.

Because of the ongoing specialisation of the economy, the Saarland has

become something of a problem child for the Bundesrepublik. Yet there is hope; the Völklinger Hütte is a good example of how new impetus can be pumped into the structurally weak Saarland, affording the state new possibilities for cultural, socio-historical and – to a certain extent – financial gain. Good luck! ■

The sound of the bell ringing at the Göttelborn pit (top left) may soon be a thing of the past; the underground miner's days are numbered (top centre). The blast room at the Völklingen works (top right) already echoes to the sound of silence.

The crude steel railway in Völklingen (bottom left) is now little more than a museum exhibit. These slag heaps (bottom right) pay sad homage to a past boom in industry.

Völklingen towers: the Church of St. Eligius (top left) and the old town hall in the industrial town (top right).

The old Völklinger Hütte has recovered a little of its former glory by being made a UNESCO World Heritage Site (main photo). The winding tower and the qualified miner in the pit (bottom left) look back to the laborious, dangerous days of work underground.

AT A GLANCE

1 Adler Post

This **country restaurant** with its beer garden serves all kinds of tasty dishes and delicious regional cuisine. The Dietzen family stage a **brunch** every last Sunday in the month based on a certain theme. The restaurant has a **schnapps distillery with a shop** where you can taste some of the produce and partake in schnapps seminars.
*(Gerlfangen, Zur Bergheck 3.
Open 11 a.m. – 2 p.m. and from 6 p.m.
Closed Mon. & Tues. p.m. Reservations
desired. Tel.: +49-(0) 68 33–5 33)*

2 Sandstone caves

The university town of **Homburg** is in the heart of the Saar-Palatinate. Atop **Karlsberg** (which is also the name of Homburg's famous beer) are the remains of the largest country residence in Europe. In the nature park on Schloßberg the medieval ruins of Homburg Castle and **Europe's largest artificial red sandstone caves** are well worth a visit.
*(Schloßberg, open daily 9 a.m. – 12 p.m.
& 1 – 5 p.m.)*

The Romans are coming! The Roman Festival at Schwarzenacker Open-Air Museum.

3 Schwarzenacker Open-Air Museum

Remains of a Roman centre of trade can be viewed in the **Römermuseum Schwarzenacker**. Parts of the buildings have been reconstructed and illustrate over **2,000 years of Homburg history**.
*(Homburg. Open Apr. – Nov.
Tues. – Sun. 9 a.m. – 12 p.m.
& 1 – 5 p.m.,
Dec. – Mar. 9 a.m. – 4.30 p.m.,
Sat., Sun. & bank hols.
12 – 4.30 p.m.)*

4 Gollenstein

The **largest menhir in Central Europe** stands proud in Blieskastel, a "state-approved" Kneipp spa town. The pretty old town with its palace and town hall is under a preservation order.

Perspectives du théâtre français

Perspectives performances take place each year in May in disused factories or outside on the streets and squares of Saarbrücken. **Experimental French theatre** has been a regular feature in the state capital's festival calendar for over 20 years now.
(City info.: tel. +49-(0) 68 1-3 69 01)

5 Peterberg

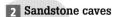

There's fun for young and old at the almost **3,000-foot-long summer tobog-gan run** on Peterberg near Braunshausen. In winter the hill is commandeered by **winter sports fanatics**. While you're here it's worth making a short detour to the **Celtic hill fort** near Otzenhausen and to the **first Southwest German Planet Trail** (Planeten-Lehrpfad) in Nonnweiler. *(Summer toboggan run: open Apr. – Oct. Wed. & Sat. 1 – 6 p.m. Sun. & bank hols. 10 a.m. – 6 p.m. Open daily during summer school holidays 10 a.m. – 6 p.m.)*

6 Restaurant Hubertus

Hubertus gourmet restaurant boasts a Michelin star and serves top-class **French cuisine**. *(Tholey, Metzer Straße 1. Hot food served daily 12 – 2 p.m. & 7 – 10 p.m. Closed Mon., Thurs. noon and Sun. p.m.; Tel.: +49-(0) 68 53-91 03-0)*

7 Roman remains

The biggest, best-preserved Roman **mosaic floor** north of the Alps measures over 1,700 square feet and was discovered in **Perl-Nennig**.
(Perl-Nennig. Open Oct. – Mar. 9 a.m. – 12 p.m. & 1 – 4.30 p.m., Apr. – Sep. 8.30 a.m. – 12 p.m. & 1 – 6 p.m. Closed Dec. & Mon.)
Not far from Nennig is the excavated Roman villa at **Perl-Borg**.
The **reconstructed baths** with their warm, cold and tepid pools are of especial interest.
(Perl–Borg. Open Tues. – Fri. 10 a.m. – 5 p.m., Sat. 11 a.m. – 8 p.m., Sun. & bank hols. 11 a.m. – 8 p.m. Closed Mon.)

8 Gasthaus Stiefel, Saarbrücken

In the traditional **Stiefel Bräu** pub-brewery on St. Johanner Markt you can see how beer is brewed and try some excellent local food.
The kitchens in the complex's **Zum Stiefel** pub offer a broad range of dishes, and in the summer the pub has a beer garden in the heart of the old town.
(Saarbrücken, Am Stiefel 2. Tel.: +49-(0) 68 1-93 64 5-0)

Saarland-Rundwanderweg

You can cover around **170 miles** on foot or on your bike on this **cycle and hiking track**. From **Saarbrücken** you go through **Homburg, St. Wendel** and past Bostal Lake to **Orscholz** and **Völklingen** before coming back to where you started: once round the Saarland. Even if you only do part of the route, you can still enjoy the Saarland in all its splendour.
(Saarwald-Verein e.V., Reichsstraße 4, D-66111 Saarbrücken. Tel.: +40-(0) 68 1-39 95 54)

9 Schloss Ziegelberg

The museum at Schloss Ziegelberg has ceramic products spanning two centuries and information on the **history of ceramics** and the **Villeroy & Boch** company.
(Mettlach. Open daily Apr. – Oct. 10 a.m. – 1 p.m. & 2 – 5 p.m., Nov. – Mar. closed Mon., Sun. & bank hols.)

10 Völklinger Hütte

The Völklinger Hütte iron and steel works has been a **UNESCO World Heritage Site** since 1994. Regular tours are offered by expert guides. **Schichtwechsel**, the two-week arts festival which takes place each year in late summer in the blast room (Gebläsehaus), is also of interest.
(Tours daily except Mon. at 10 a.m. & 2 p.m. Closed Jan., Feb. & Dec. Tel.: +49-(0) 68 98-2 77 34)

11 Wolfspark

In Kammerforst Forest in **Merzig** Werner Freund studies the behaviour of his **grey wolves** in their outdoor enclosure. You can watch Freund with his animals every first Sunday in the month from 4 p.m. onwards. Free entrance.
(Merzig. Open daily until dark. Tours by arrangement only. Tel.: +49-(0) 68 61-10 51)

Tourist Information

Further information is available from Tourismus-Zentrale Saarland (TZS), Franz-Josef-Röder-Straße 9, 66119 Saarbrücken;
Tel.: +49-(0) 6 81-92 72 00, fax -92 72 04-0.

Top left: Roman mosaic in Nennig. Centre: Schloss Ziegelberg Museum.

World Heritage Site Völklinger Hütte: the blast furnace with the ore conveyor.

1 11
The numbers 1 – 11 refer to positions marked on the map on pages 2 – 3

CHRONOLOGICAL TABLE

400 The Romans are unable to continue to defend their territories on the Saar against hoards of advancing Teutonic tribes. Franks dominate the area.

890 Royal Sarabrucca Castle, built on a rock which drops steeply down to the river, is said to mark the founding of Saarbrücken. In 999 Emperor Otto III gives the castle to the bishop of Metz.

Relics from the French period: canons in frontof the casemates in Saarlouis (below).

Right: plan of Vauban Fortress in Saarlouis.

1321 Count John I issues a "Writ of Freedom" to the "town of Saarbrücken and the village of St. Johann". Saarbrücken and St. Johann become "municipalities with shared legal and administrative bodies".

1381 Saarbrücken is made the capital of the earldom of Saarbrücken (part of Nassau).

1503 St. Johann is decimated by fire and the Plague and thus falls behind Saarbrücken in its development.

1604 Count Louis, a keen patron of the sciences, opens a school in Saarbrücken for "the education of citizens' sons".

1617 Count Louis's Renaissance palace in Saarbrücken is completed, one of the most sumptuous princely residences in southwest Germany.

1635 During the Thirty Years' War Duke Bernhard of Weimar's army, fighting for the Swedes, occupies Saarbrücken with the help of French troops.

1641 Emperor Ferdinand III pledges the earldom of Saarbrücken and Homburg Fortress to the Duke of Lorraine. The population is oppressed and threatened.

1644 The French march into Saarbrücken.

1685 Sun King Louis XIV has Saarlouis (Sarrelouis) turned into a riverside fortress.

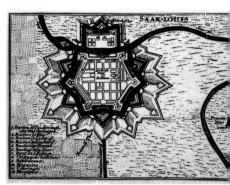

1762–1775 Prince William Henry creates an impressive Baroque ensemble in the centre of Saarbrücken with the Ludwigskirche and Ludwigsplatz (his architect is Friedrich Joachim Stengel).

1801 Saarbrücken falls to France. 14 years later the Prussians gain control of the Saarland.

1870 The Saarland is taken by the French on August 2 during the Franco-Prussian War but is liberated at the battle in the Spicher Hills four days later.

1909 Alt-Saarbrücken, St. Johann and Malstatt-Burbach merge to form the city of Saarbrücken. St. Arnual is joined with Alt-Saarbrücken in 1896.

1920 In the aftermath of the First World War the Saar Territory (Bassin de la Sarre) falls under the administration of the League of Nations.

1935 An overwhelming majority of the Saar's inhabitants vote to again be part of Germany.

1945 Following the Second World War the Saarland is once more subject to French rule.

1947 The "autonomous" Saarland launches its own state parliament. The region, economically affiliated to France, acquires sections of the Trier, Saarburg and Kusel districts. Customs posts exercise strict control over the roads leading to and from Germany. The University of the Saarland is founded in Saarbrücken and Homburg.

1955 On October 23 the majority of the Saar populace votes against the Saarland becoming a European statute and thus inaugurates the region's return to Germany.

The tower of Saarbrücken's old town hall (top left) and a museum truck in Völklingen.

1957 The Saarland is economically united with Germany.

1959 The Saarland joins Germany's federal system of states and becomes a Bundesland.

1994 The Völklinger Hütte iron and steel works is made a UNESCO World Heritage Site.

1997 The Saarland celebrates 50 years of its constitution and state parliament.

The tallest winding tower still in operation in Europe stands proud with its disk wheels above Göttelborn.

INDEX

A	Text/*Picture*
Adler Post (country restaurant), Gerlfangen 64/	

B
Bischmisheim.../29
Bliesbruck...30/31
Blieskastel..12, 64/26, 29
Borg (Perl)..31, 65/31
Bostal Lake.....................................15 /15, 37
Burg Montclair ..../50

G
Göttelborn 60, 61/11, 60, 61, 67
Gollenstein (Blieskastel) 12, 64/27

H
Homburg...64–67/28, 64
Hubertus (restaurant), Tholey.........................64/

L
Losheim (Losheim Lake) ..../17, 47
Louis XIV (Sun King) 14, 66/

M
Maybach../14, 17
Max Ophüls Festival, Saarbrücken 22/
Merzig 17, 65/45, 54, 65
Mettlach......................12, 52, 53, 65/50–53, 65

N
Nennig (Perl)..........................17, 31, 65/13, 31, 65
Neunkirchen ..../14, 32, 33, 60
Niederwürzbach ..../28
Nonnweiler..15, 46, 64/16

O
Ophüls, Max..22/22
Orscholz (bow in the River Saar) 12, 65/48
Ottweiler../36
Otzenhausen...13, 64/

P
Perl...45, 65/
Perspectives du théâtre français,
Saarbrücken.....................................23, 64/22, 23
Peterberg (Braunshausen)................64/40, 42, 64

R	Text/*Picture*
Roman remains ....30, 31 /30, 31	

S
Saarbrücken 14, 22, 23, 64–67/13, 17–25, 67
 - Ludwigskirche 66/21
 - Max Ophüls Festival 22/
 - Palace...66/8
 - Perspectives 23, 64/22, 23
 - St. Arnual's 67/20
 - St. Johanner Markt 15/15, 19
 - Staatstheater.../18
 - University ..../4
 - Weinstube Hauck../45
 - Zum Stiefel (brewery)............................15, 65/

Sarreguemines (Saargemünd)..........17/10, 24, 25
Saarlouis 14, 17, 66/56, 57, 66
Saar (bow in the river near Orscholz)...........12/48
Saar contracts..38, 39/39
Schloss Saarfels ..../45
St. Wendel 16, 17, 65/34, 35
Schloss Berg 31/50
Schloss Ziegelberg (Mettlach) 53, 65/65
Schwarzenacker (Homburg) 64/64, 30
Sculpture Trail (St. Wendel) 16/
Spellenstein (Rentrisch)................................12/12
Stones along the Border Project (Merzig) 16/55
Stiefel (Rentrisch) ..../27

T
Theley ..../36
Tholey 16, 64/37

Ü, V
Überherrn ..../54
Villeroy & Boch 52, 53/50, 52, 53
Völklingen
(Völklinger Hütte) 61, 65, 67/58, 61–63, 65, 67

W
Wadern.../42, 46
Waldhölzbach.../47
Walhausen...12/
Weiskirchen.../43

The Schlosskirche, situated in a
quiet corner of Saarbrücken,
is spared the drone of city traffic.

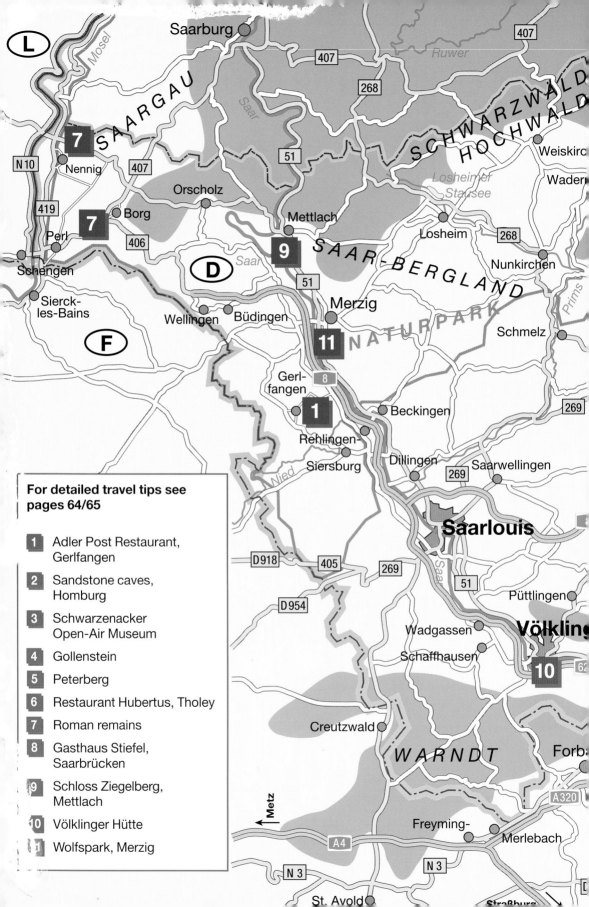

L

Saarburg

407

Ruwer

407

268

S A A R G A U

Mosel

7

N 10

Nennig

407

Saar

51

S C H W A R Z W A L D
H O C H W A L D

Weiskirc

Wader

Losheimer
Stausee

419

7

Borg

406

Orscholz

Mettlach

9

S A A R - B E R G L A N D

Losheim

268

Nunkirchen

Perl

Schengen

Saar

D

Merzig

Schmelz

Sierck-
les-Bains

Wellingen

Büdingen

11

N A T U R P A R K

Prims

F

Gerl-
fangen

8

1

Beckingen

269

Rehlingen-
Siersburg

Wied

Dillingen

Saarwellingen

269

For detailed travel tips see
pages 64/65

1 Adler Post Restaurant,
   Gerlfangen

2 Sandstone caves,
   Homburg

3 Schwarzenacker
   Open-Air Museum

4 Gollenstein

5 Peterberg

6 Restaurant Hubertus, Tholey

7 Roman remains

8 Gasthaus Stiefel,
   Saarbrücken

9 Schloss Ziegelberg,
   Mettlach

10 Völklinger Hütte

11 Wolfspark, Merzig

Saarlouis

D918

405

269

51

Püttlingen

D954

Wadgassen

Völkling

Schaffhausen

10

62

Creutzwald

W A R N D T

Forb

Metz

A320

Freyming-

A4

Merlebach

N 3

N 3

St. Avold

Straßburg

Stürtz-REGIO –
Practical, packed with
illustrations – great souvenirs.
Stürtz Verlag GmbH,
Beethovenstraße 5,
D-97080 Würzburg